ENERGY DIET

How to eat for maximum daily energy

Harry Livingstone

© **Copyright 2019 by Harry Livingstone - All rights reserved.**

This document is geared towards providing exact and reliable information in regards to the topic and issue covered. The publication is sold with the idea that the publisher is not required to render accounting, officially permitted, or otherwise, qualified services. If advice is necessary, legal or professional, a practiced individual in the profession should be ordered.

From a Declaration of Principles which was accepted and approved equally by a Committee of the American Bar Association and a Committee of Publishers and Associations.

In no way is it legal to reproduce, duplicate, or transmit any part of this

document in either electronic means or in printed format. Recording of this publication is strictly prohibited and any storage of this document is not allowed unless with written permission from the publisher. All rights reserved.

The information provided herein is stated to be truthful and consistent, in that any liability, in terms of inattention or otherwise, by any usage or abuse of any policies, processes, or directions contained within is the solitary and utter responsibility of the recipient reader. Under no circumstances will any legal responsibility or blame be held against the publisher for any reparation, damages, or monetary loss due to the information herein, either directly or indirectly.

The information herein is offered for informational purposes solely, and is universal as so. The presentation of the information is without contract or any type of guarantee assurance.

The trademarks that are used are without any consent, and the publication of the trademark is without permission or backing by the trademark owner. All trademarks and brands within this book are for clarifying purposes only and are the owned by the owners themselves, not affiliated with this document.

INTRODUCTION

I want to thank you and congratulate you for downloading the book '**ENERGY DIET**'.

This book contains proven steps and strategies on how to eat for maximum daily energy.

We feed ourselves according to the hunger signals in our brain that translate to signals in our body. For most of us this happens at least 3 times a day and then some. But unless we keep a journal or document it, we forget or don't even care what we have eaten during the day. We then begin to feel extreme fatigue, lack of concentration, low productivity at work, sleeplessness, weight gain, and more. When these counter-productive symptoms kick in, we begin to pay attention to them and find our bodies behavior extremely confusing.

This book will enable you to look at how you are eating each and every day so that you can see EXACTLY what is causing your unwanted symptoms. You can correct most symptoms quickly!

This book is centered on the fact that by eating raw foods you can avail the most amount of nutrition out of your diet. By eating raw foods, you consume all of the healthy nutrients such as food enzymes, minerals, and vitamins in their purest form. It is a very well known proven fact that cooking food changes its chemistry and many essential nutrients are lost in the process.

Also in this book, you will find the importance of consuming good quality protein, great fat (s), and complex carbohydrates in every meal you eat throughout the day. Protein such as organic poultry, fish, organic low-fat and nonfat dairy, very lean meat (used sparingly), plus seeds, avocados, olive and grapeseed oil, and WHOLE GRAIN breads and cereals for maximum daily energy.

Thanks again for downloading this book, I hope you enjoy it!

TABLE OF CONTENTS

INTRODUCTION i

CHAPTER 1: INCREASED ENERGY DIET 1

   Easy Ways To Boost and Sustain Your Energy Level 2

   Why Many Diets Don't Work 6

CHAPTER 2: EAT TO BUILD MUSCLES EFFECTIVELY ... 12

CHAPTER 3: EAT TO BOOST YOUR ENERGY 18

   Boosting Your Energy Level by Eating Healthy 18

   5 Power Foods For a High-Energy Diet 24

CHAPTER 4: THE ENERGY 'DIET' 28

   How to Boost Your Energy Level Without Caffeine or Other Stimulants 32

CHAPTER 5: BOOST YOUR ENERGY WITH COMPLEX CARBOHYDRATES IN YOUR DIET 35

   What are Carbohydrates? 36

   Complex Carbohydrates as Energy 39

CHAPTER 6: RAW FOOD DIET 41

   How to Adopt a Raw Food Diet 47

CONCLUSION 52

CHAPTER 1

INCREASED ENERGY DIET

In today's society, everyone is expected to do more with less. The cost of living is increasing exponentially faster than the rate of salary increase. Companies are asking staff to increase productivity with less resources. Gone are the days when one parent was able to stay home to raise their children and handle household duties. Both parents are working outside of the home for a majority of the day and still raising children while trying to maintain their homelife. Students are bombarded with significantly more information than their parents and grandparents were presented with during their school years, usually within the same number of annual school days to process the information. Yet, we do not have more hours in the day to be more productive. What is the result? People are tired. It seems everyone is looking for ways to boost their energy levels so that they can meet the demands of life.

You should avoid many types of energy drinks and pills, stay healthy, and get more energy at the same time. All you have to do is eat the right foods, exercise and supplement with healthy choices.

There are many diets that claim to give you more energy. You should be careful before jumping on board and signing up for new eating habits. They can be costly and not all diets out there may be worth it in the end. Do the appropriate amount of research for each diet to decide if one is right for you. Make sure to check reviews online, consult friends that have dietary knowledge and do your homework before embarking on a new eating routine. You can learn so much just by conversing with someone that's already been down that dietary rabbit hole. Don't let your goal of achieving more energy push you abruptly into dubious diets found online or elsewhere. There are many healthy foods and exercises that you can get yourself to wake yourself up. The answer is usually relatively simple when it comes to your body and diet!

Easy Ways To Boost and Sustain Your Energy Level

When looking for a natural boost of energy, or when wondering why you are often lethargic, diet is the first place to look. One must make sure that the level of processed foods consumed are kept to a minimum. Processed foods in your pantry are usually recognized as foods that do not expire or begin to perish within a couple of months. Processed foods appear in the forms of cereals, chips, microwave popcorn, candy, ready made desserts, etc. Processed food in your refrigerator and freezer are foods that are not in their natural state. Examples are lunch meats, chicken nuggets, hot dogs, many dairy products, sausages, packaged sauces, condiments, bread, etc. It is helpful to get into the habit of reading the ingredients of your packaged food as to educate yourself on everyday food items. If the contents are a myriad of many dubious unrecognizable and unpronounceable ingredients than as a rule of thumb, you probably should refrain from putting it in your body! Everything we need to nourish and energize our bodies is already growing naturally on the earth. The human body has not yet evolved to the point of capably processing and eliminating manufactured and harmful ingredients. Consuming said ingredients have been proven to lead to all types of health issues, fatigue being one of them.

Eliminating as many artificial ingredients from the diet is a potentially life-changing first step to becoming a more energetic you, so that productivity can be increased and activities enjoyed thoroughly. However, there are appropriate times when an immediate boost of energy is needed to make it through the evening exercise class, finishing up a project, or even an all night study session. Caffeine is a great source of energy and does have some health benefits. However, caffeinated drinks and energy drinks often contain unhealthy and potentially harmful ingredients when consumed over the long term. Coffee and tea provide a healthy dose of caffeine with no harmful side effects when consumed by themselves. However, what can make coffee and tea as unhealthy as the other energy drinks are the sweeteners, toppings and creamers. Keeping sugar and cream to a minimum is a must if you are to naturally gain control over your energy levels. You will experience an energy crash later in the day once the sugar rush wears off from these sweeteners and creamers. Caffeine is available in other forms besides beverages, which can be consumed without the calories from added sugar and other ingredients. Certain vitamin supplements are also an excellent answer to a much-needed energy boost.

In order to be more productive in a smaller amount of time, more energy and focus is required. We have all tried at one time or another, to sludge our way through the important work or school project, when all our bodies want to do is lie down and take a nap! Take a look at the kind of food you are regularly consuming if chronic fatigue is a problem in your life. For a quick boost of energy, you may want to seriously consider staying away from sugary energy drinks and making them a beverage choice of the past. Caffeinated coffee and tea work well and are healthy as long as the cream andsugar is kept to a minimum. Caffeine and vitamin supplements are a handy go-to in situations where there is no access to coffee or tea. I have kept these supplements handy when traveling long distances and a project deadline is impending.

Of course, coffee is the classic go-to-drink when it comes to fatigue. This is due to the fact that of all natural foods, coffee has the highest level of caffeine. Caffeine has been proven to improve your performance and decrease your perception of effort involved with the task in hand, which can allow you to work harder for longer. It also has its wonderful natural aroma going for it!

Fruits are a great source of energy; especially apricots,

bananas, cantaloupe, and kiwi. These fruits are high in potassium, fructose for liver glycogen, ready-to-use sugars, fiber, and tons of vitamins, minerals and antioxidants. Consuming fruits throughout the day will provide you with the occasional natural boost of energy. You can also blend fruits together with Greek frozen yogurt for a healthy and tasty snack.

Old-fashioned oats are a good source of complex carbohydrates that are high in fiber, low on the glycemic index and high in B vitamins that boost energy. Unlike instant oatmeal, old-fashioned oats are a natural, unprocessed form of the oat.

Seeds from flax, chia and hemp provide you with a lot of fiber, healthy fats, vitamins, minerals, and antioxidants. Chia is an excellent choice because it contains a lot of soluble fiber, which creates a viscous gel in your gastrointestinal tract. Seeds are a wonderful addition to a morning smoothie.

Omega-3 eggs have a lot of healthy fats, energy-boosting B vitamins and vitamin D. They also contain choline, the precursor for acetylcholine, and are a great protein because of their amino acid profile and high biological value.

As you can gather, there is a whole world of healthy foods you can consume to gain more daily energy. Don't let the stress of your busy day suck the energy out of you. Start a diet with increased energy by eating the best healthy foods, getting plenty of exercise, drinking 6 to 8 glasses of water daily and making sure you are getting 6 to 8 hours of sleep each night.

You have heard this advice time and time again, but the time has come to put it into action! Take responsibility for your energy levels starting today!

Why Many Diets Don't Work

Diets are often associated with weight loss, however, weight loss is not the only desired dietary result. The desired outcomes of diets range from better sleep, a reduced body fat percentage, victory in fitness competitions, allergies, weight gain, climate change concerns, animal rights, fighting depression and anxiety, and gaining more daily energy (the inspiration behind this book!). There are a seemingly endless amount of reasons for one to partake in a certain diet. Weight loss is just one example. A reason for many people's failure to gain successful results from their diet is not always the diet itself being faulty or a scam, but it is often the individual's work-ethic, approach, execution and discipline pertaining to the diet that warrants how successful their outcomes are. With the many diets out there, there are countless individuals that simply just have a hard time following-up and maintaining the necessary discipline needed to adhere to a strict diet. The result is that ones chosen diet is not a transforming catalyst for lifestyle change. The change must first happen within oneself. One must commit to their chosen diet and not allow temptation to sway them from their end game or final result!

The helpful transformative methods I have used on my dietary journeys vary. Before I embark on my chosen diet I take these simple steps; Firstly, I write down my diet goals. I write a long term (approximately one year) and short term (approximately one month) desired outcomes. Underneath these desired outcomes I will make a note of target weights I would like to hit and any details of body mass or target body fat percentages. Next, I will write down how I will achieve these goals. This is an integral step in my process. The 'how I will achieve my goals' section will cover essential information such as what I will eat and drink, what juices I will prepare and consume (if any) and what supplements will aid me. I will also add an additional section covering sleep goals (7 hours of uninterrupted sleep per night, subconscious affirmations playing quietly in headphones during sleep to program my subconscious mind. This is intended to fully immerse myself in the diet and to build discipline etc) and exercise goals (how often I will work out, what exercises or/and sports I will participate in etc). This additional goal section is intended to help me with any peripheral factors that may aid in my diet's success and fast track my results. Sleep and exercise are arguably as important as the diet itself and these factors cannot be ignored!

Following my goal setting, I will mark down WHY I want to succeed on my dietary journey. You must have a strong reason why you want to succeed if you want to see results and gain the essential discipline. The potential reasons for why one wants to achieve success in their diet are endless. Take a minute to think about and jot down your reasons for changing your current diet or temporarily trying a new diet.

Are you worried about your health? Do you want to attract that new man or woman into your life? Do you want to come first place in that fitness competition? Do you want to live longer and be there for your kids or grandkids? Or do you want more energy to get that big work project completed before the deadline? Whatever your reason(s), writing down your 'why(s)' and sticking them on your wall or bathroom mirror to see every day will give you that added push to achieve success! You must also ask yourself, what is the result of staying in my current habits? If you regularly eat unhealthy foods then ask yourself, what kinds of illnesses could I likely suffer from in the future? How many goals will go unaccomplished if I lack the energy to complete them? What happens if I don't attract that man or woman into my life? Look deep inside of yourself and find the answers to any of your questions that come up. Write down the questions and answers and review them on a regular basis to enrich you with added power and inspiration to achieve your dietary goals! There is simply no area of your life that a new, healthier diet will not improve! Change your life starting with your diet today!

Finally, I will journal my daily results, habits, and activities. This is an essential step as you will be able to pinpoint any areas of your diet that could perhaps be interchanged with different, more beneficial habits. Perhaps you are sleeping too long and it is making you lethargic. Perhaps you are fasting throughout the day and then gorging on unhealthy treats during the evening, an issue then can be resolved by not going too many hours without eating. I recommend organic unsalted almonds as a healthy snack between meals. If the diet is intended to boost daily energy, then I will write out a one to ten scale of how much energy I feel daily and journal this on the pages following my goals. If my energy is regularly being marked down under a five or six, then I know something has to change. I will pinpoint what needs to change by thoroughly reviewing what I have been eating, drinking and how I have been exercising and sleeping.

Another helpful method I often use to keep me on track with my diets is a vision board. You may have seen many successful people create vision boards and hang them up on the wall as a constant reminder for their 'why' and to boost them with daily inspiration to achieve their goals. Many entrepreneurs will create vision boards littered with images of their dream cars, houses, and accomplishments. This manifestation and inspiration fueling method has helped millions of people achieve financial, artistic and relationship success, but it doesn't end there. You can create your own vision board to aid you in your dietary journey. You may consider adding images of your dream body, or that dream male or female you would like to attract into your life. You may also want to add images of that trophy you will receive when you get first place in that fitness competition or that black belt you will receive from triumphing in your martial arts class. Hopefully, this section has inspired you to work on methods for boosting your inspiration to help you stick with your diet. Remember, a diet is not just the food you eat. This is only part of it, to be successful in your diet you must make your mindset, beliefs and habits just as important as the foods you are consuming.

Once your dietary goal is achieved, you must maintain your new healthier habits. Many dieters revert to their old eating habits and lifestyle and hence end up feeling just as lethargic, depressed or unfit as they did pre-diet. This counterproductive reversion can lead to old weight being re-gained and old health issues returning. Dietary undoing can mean a range of returning issues depending on the diet. For example, someone on a diabetic diet could become very sick if they do not follow through and maintain their diet. An individual attempting to gain muscle could lose their progress and someone trying to become healthy and stay on an energy diet could suffer an energy crash and begin to once again experience constant fatigue.

The key to sticking to a diet or change in eating patterns is as simple as a person's will power. Low will power is a common reason why many people decide that embarking on a year long diet to lose weight is less likely to succeed versus a more dramatic short-term diet that will result (in their minds) in more drastic, faster results, hence many of the diet fads and 'overnight' promises from many 'lose weight quick' companies. Some of these dietary methods can be dangerous so make sure the company/method is reputable and you have read plenty of reviews before trying it out! Think of your diet as a marathon, not a sprint. Maintaining your results and health is as important as initially achieving the results themselves. The marathon approach mindset will help you sustain your health and diet for longer time periods after you have have achieved your main goal or target weight etc. As remaining on a diet becomes more difficult and less fun, the individual can often begin to lose interest and eventually go into a form of relapse. The results of which are unwanted based on the initial effort to lose weight or live healthily. This is an important fact to take note of for anyone going forward with a chosen a diet. While will power is different in everyone, the resolve to meet goals can be bolstered by support groups, that include family and friends, facebook groups, fitness or martial arts/sports classes, individuals on the same type of diet and even a personal counselor or lifestyle coach. Books and online resources are also encouraged to help improve your dietary knowledge and equip you with different exercises that will help you fast track your goals. We live in a day and age where each one of us that owns a smartphone has more information then the president of the United States would have had immediate access to twenty years ago! This is an outrageous but true fact. There is simply no excuse for not supplying yourself with and seeking out the necessary information for you to take control of your dietary habits and every other area of your life! You are incredibly lucky to live in this day and age where an abundance of knowledge is at your fingertips. Whether the knowledge comes from online courses, youtube, Skype sessions with a fitness coach or e-books like this one you are reading right now, use it to your advantage!

CHAPTER 2

EAT TO BUILD MUSCLES EFFECTIVELY

Your gym routine is a determining factor in wether you will achieve maximum energy in your daily life. Cardio is viewed by many as the holy grail of energy boosting work outs. Although weight lifting can tire you out for the day depending on how heavy and how hard you go, it is essential to add (even a light) weight routine into your gym work out. There is such a thing as too much cardio. Think of your gym routine as being like a healthy well rounded diet also! Building even a small amount of muscle or getting fit and toned will contribute to your overall health and energy in life changing amounts. It will even release endorphins and bring about a sense of happiness and well being. Well rounded work outs are a win win!

When you are training in the gym in order to build muscle mass, the effectiveness of the muscle growth depends on the training intensity and the amount of building material that you nourish your body with. Structures like joints, tendons and bones will also grow to support larger muscles. These body parts will also need building materials found in your diet. This growth occurs around the clock, day or night, although it is widely believed that most of this growth occurs during sleeping hours. To really have your results thrive, you must supply your body with a constant reserve of building materials (nutrients) that are absorbed through your system. In addition, the body needs nutrients to repair wearing in the tissues, not unlike a child or teen needing essential nutrients (building blocks) for their healthy growth. You must also supply your body with reserves of energy for these training activities that can transition over to energize you for any additional regular daily activities.

The necessary building materials for muscles and supporting structures are mostly found in protein based foods and supplements, but also in lecithin, essential fatty acids, calcium, magnesium, and other minerals. When building muscle, aim for the food you consume to give you protein with an amino acid composition that will support your muscles as much as possible. Fish, poultry, lean meat, eggs, mushrooms, seafood and diary products are good protein sources for muscle growth. Just before training, it is best to consume proteins that you can easily digest and absorb, like in fish, eggs and seafood. Protein-rich foods such as red meat and eggs, however, may diminish energy levels throughout the day. Red meat may stay in the digestive tract for long periods of time and cause lethargy. Aim for protein-rich foods such as fish and seafood instead. These foods will excel in muscle growth, enhance brain function and boost energy!

Much of your energy intake should be from carbohydrates,

mostly starch, that is absorbed into your system and digested slowly. Full cornbread and cereals, peas, beans and potatoes are good carbohydrate sources with this digestive trait. Some of your energy can also be supplied with healthy fats, which is a combination of chemically unaltered monounsaturated fat, omega-3-fat and omega-6-fat. Healthy fats will also be absorbed slowly through your digestive system and release a steady burn of energy. Good fat sources are found in fish, almonds, avocado, sunflower seeds, coconut oil, olive oil, rapeseed oil and flax oil. The slow uptake of these energy sources gives you an even supply of energy all throughout the day.

Slow, steady burning energy sources aside, there are also occasions that you may desire a boost of energy that strikes quickly and powerfully, perhaps before a gym training session, a study session, or a big exam. Sugar has a somewhat negative reputation due to its harmful effects to health over time, not to mention the dental ordeals that one might be subjected to after too great an intake! But, we must not forget the potential energy packed into sugar. This can periodically be helpful in the aforementioned scenarios. Good sources of sugar are sweet fruit and fruit juices. Carbohydrate concentrates especially made for training can also be used. Try to use sugar strategically and don't let this be a part of your regular routine. I limit myself to a small amount of fruit per day in my morning smoothies. Overdoing it with processed sugars can result in an energy crash later in the day and future pounds being packed on that you will need to lose in the gym.

A meal plan for maximum muscle growth will differ from the traditional diet you will find in any country. Contrary to popular belief, it is not always necessary to eat a high quantity of meals every day to receive a constant supply of nutrients. This is because what you eat during each meal will stay in your digestive system and be utilized in the following hours. How much you eat should depend upon your training intensity and your activity level. It is important to eat so that you feel comfortably full at each meal, but not so that you are bloated and lethargic. As a rule of thumb, try not to eat a larger volume of food than your balled-up fist. As you surpass this volume of food, your stomach will have to expand and work harder to digest it.

Here is a meal plan for the implementation of the aforementioned principles based on the 4 meal per day approach. It is possible, however, to distribute the same amount of food in 5 or 6 smaller meals throughout the day if you wish.

- Early each day, eat a meal composed of three principal parts in an equal amount. One part consists of protein rich elements like fish, lean meat, eggs, seafood, poultry, lean cheese or mushrooms. The other part consists of food types rich in carbohydrate or fat such as full corn bread, peas, beans, potatoes, almonds, sunflower seeds, and some plant oils. Try to compose this part so that you get more carbohydrates and less fat. The third part is vegetables and fruit, preferably raw. This will help you to burn steady

energy with the nutrients from these foods for several hours.
- Later in the day, try eating a meal with a similar composition, but which varies from the other food sources consumed in the morning. This will secure an even supply of nutrients that will keep you going until evening.
- In the evening, you can try to eat mostly protein rich foods, and less foods rich in carbohydrates and fat. Try to eat other food types than you ate earlier in the day to take advantage of the variation in nutrients. You should always make an effort to have a rather large portion of vegetables and fruit in this meal. This meal ensures you get enough material to grow muscles during night, but less energy than the earlier meals. This is because you do not need so much energy when you are getting ready to sleep.
- Just before training, you should eat a smaller meal with proteins and carbohydrates that your body can easily absorb during digestion. You can base this meal upon fish or seafood, very sweet fruit and fruit juice, which all are easily accessible and quick to consume on the go. You may also use protein and carbohydrate concentrates in this meal. A supply of lecithin, minerals and essential fatty acids will also be useful at this time.

Depending on your training session time, this meal may come at varied times of the day, on different days of the week. If you train at a time when you ordinarily should eat one of the main meals, you can simply just schedule your main meal to earlier or later that day.

All meals should be accompanied by sufficient liquids to help digestion and ensure that you are hydrated. It is recommended to chug plenty of water upon waking as you will be very dehydrated after 7 or more hours of sleep from the night before. Chugging water first thing after waking in the morning on an empty stomach will kickstart your metabolism and give you a boost of energy as the cells of your body become hydrated! Always consume plenty of water during training. Make sure to avoid a lot of added salt and sugar in your beverages and avoid snacks, cakes and sweets in significant amounts that may be packaged or advertised as work out aids. The unhealthy ingredients in many of these products are likely to pack on sneaky pounds behind the scenes and leave you scratching your head, wondering why you are not losing the weight!

CHAPTER 3

EAT TO BOOST YOUR ENERGY

Boosting Your Energy Level by Eating Healthy

A great, healthy breakfast will boost your concentration and kick start your energy levels. Keep your body energized with complex carbohydrates. Foods with a high level of Vitamin B are great producers of energy. The key is to keep a steady level of energy all day with a healthy diet. You must eliminate all sugary breakfast cereals, donuts and sweet foods of this nature. If you eat these foods then you are heading for a midday sugar crash! Lethargy will be your constant sidekick if you choose to start your day with these foods!

We are going to discuss when you should eat, and the best foods during what time of day. Other things you need to ask yourself are why are you eating? What are you eating? And where are you eating?

Breakfast being the most important meal of the day means you should consume some type of protein. This meal starts your day and proteins give off energy as they are digested. Try low fat yogurt or cottage cheese. Also, whole grain cereals with low fat milk are a great way to start your day. My favorite source of morning protein is vegan, unsweetened protein powder added into a healthy morning green smoothie. Vegan protein powder is relatively inexpensive and can be found in most grocery stores and supermarkets. If its something sweet you crave in the mornings then you can sweeten up your breakfast in a healthy way with some fruit! I recommend organic fruit so as to avoid any harmful pesticides that perhaps may have been dispersed amongst the growing fruits.

We all know not everyone is on a three meal a day diet. If you are a "snacker" like me, then you will want something to keep you going between meals. Studies have shown that having small meals and small snacks throughout the day is good for you. Your body is like a furnace and you must keep adding fuel to it so that it does not burn out. Eating small healthy meals and snacks helps your body utilize its nutrients more efficiently and speeds up your metabolism. Also, you will not be as hungry all the time and you won't over eat when meal time comes around. You will also be less likely to gorge on unhealthy snacks and maintain a stronger resistance against temptation.

A great mid morning snack would definitely be fruits or vegetables. These are low in fat but high in fiber choices that give you a reserve of energy. Another good option would be all natural peanut butter on wheat crackers. This gives you a protein source and a steady blood sugar level to keep you energized and full until lunch. After lunch, for your mid-afternoon snack, you can try salsa with unsalted corn tortilla chips, or dried fruit. Choose something small that will be able to satisfy you until dinner time and help you avoid a crash of fatigue.

Make sure for lunch, you do not over eat as it will cause you to feel sleepy and bring about a lethargic state that will force you to sludge your way through the rest of the day. Eating healthy, unprocessed cheeses, fish, or lean meats would be your best bet during lunch to power you through the day. These foods will raise the energy levels in your brain by increasing chemicals called catecholamines.

We have all seen and been taught about the food pyramid at school. At dinner time, remember your food pyramid. Try to approximate that seventy -five percent of your plate consists of fruits, veggies, and grains. The other twenty-five percent should consist of your meats and dairy products. If you are vegetarian or vegan then replace these meat and/or dairy products with other protein-based foods.

Don't forget about your bedtime snack. Be careful consuming too much food before you go to sleep. Over-eating before bed can effect the quality of your sleep. Some harder to digest foods such as processed cheese and chocolates have actually been said to even cause nightmares! Bad sleep equals low energy. Try grapes as they are filled with melatonin. Melatonin is a wonderful sleep aid that can also be found in pill form inexpensively.

If you are a gym-goer (as I would highly recommend) and are going to work out regularly, then you need to watch what type of meals you are consuming pre work out. Avoid eating a full meal immediately before working out, you will be too full and tired to exercise efficiently as your stomach will still be trying to move the contents of your meal into the digestive system. You must avoid stomach cramps from working out on a full stomach, this will ruin the effectiveness of your work out. Meals that are high in fat can also make you cramp, so avoid those as well. A half hour prior to exercising, eat protein for power or complex carbohydrates as they digest fast and also leave you satisfied.

Juggling the responsibilities of work, life, and family life can sometimes cause too little sleep, too much stress, and too little time. Yet, even when you're at your busiest, you should never cut corners when it comes to maintaining a healthy diet. Your body needs healthy, sustaining foods to function at its best and to fight the daily stress and fatigue of life. By dumping quick but unhealthy foods into your body, you are doing yourself and your life a huge disservice. Put in the extra effort to prepare that salad before work tomorrow, instead of chowing down that unhealthy fast food on your break. Exercise the discipline to avoid filling your coffee with creamer. Go for a run and sip on an amino acid powder supplement drink instead of zoning out in front of the tv and chugging a six-pack of beer. You will soon notice that your life will be enriched with a newfound energy and you will feel like you can handle work life and family life with ease compared to the old unhealthy you.

Energy and Diet: How The Body Turns Food Into Fuel

Our energy comes from the foods we eat and the liquids we drink. The three main nutrients our body uses for energy are carbohydrates, protein, and fats, with carbohydrates being the most important source.

Your body can also use protein and fats for energy when carbs have been depleted. When you eat, your body breaks down nutrients into smaller components and absorbs them to use as fuel. This process is known as metabolism.

Carbohydrates come in two types; simple and complex, and both are converted to sugar (glucose). "The body breaks the sugar down in the blood and the blood cells use the glucose to provide energy," says Melissa Rifkin, RD, a registered dietitian of the Montefiore Medical Center in the Bronx, N.Y.

Energy and Diet: Best Foods for Sustained Energy

Complex carbohydrates such as high-fiber cereals, whole-grain breads and pastas, dried beans, and starchy vegetables are the best type of foods for prolonged energy because they are digested at a slow, consistent rate. "Complex carbohydrates contain fiber, which takes a longer time to digest in the body as it is absorbed slowly," says Rifkin. Complex carbs also stabilize your body's sugar level, which in turn causes the pancreas to produce less insulin. This gives you a feeling of satiety and you are less hungry."

Also important in a healthy, energy-producing diet is protein (preferably chicken, turkey, pork tenderloin, and fish), legumes (lentils and beans), and a moderate amount of healthy monounsaturated and polyunsaturated fats (avocados, seeds, nuts, and certain oils).

"Adequate fluids are also essential for sustaining energy," says Suzanne Lugerner, RN, director of clinical nutrition at the Washington Hospital Center in Washington, D.C. "Water is necessary for digestion, absorption, and the transport of nutrients for energy. Dehydration can cause a lack of energy. The average person needs to drink six to eight 8-ounce glasses of water each day."

Energy and Diet: Foods to Avoid

Simple carbohydrates, on the other hand, should be limited. Ranging from candy and cookies to sugary beverages and juices, simple carbs are broken down and absorbed quickly by the body. They provide an initial burst of energy for 30 to 60 minutes but are digested so quickly that they can result in a slump afterward.

You should also avoid alcohol and caffeine if you want long sustaining energy. Alcohol is a depressant and can reduce your energy levels, while caffeine usually provides an initial two-hour energy burst, followed by a crash.

Energy and Diet: Scheduling Meals for Sustained Energy

"I always recommend three meals and three snacks a day and to never go over three to four hours without eating something," says Tara Harwood, RD, a registered dietitian at the Cleveland Clinic in Ohio. "If you become too hungry, this can cause you to overeat."

Also, try to include something from each food group at every meal, remembering that foods high in fiber, protein, and fat take a longer time to digest.

Even if your life is hectic, it's important to make wise food choices that provide energy throughout the day. Your body will thank you and you will become more productive!

5 Power Foods For a High-Energy Diet

For anyone who is undergoing an intense home workout, the secret to success is providing your body with the energy it needs not only to get through the home exercise program, but also through the rest of the day. Items such as energy bars and supplements are a good place to start. To really increase your energy output and enjoy the health benefits, include these 5 power-boosting foods in your diet every day:

1. **Bananas:** This is one of the best snacks around when it comes to raising your energy level for an intense home workout. This type of fruit contains carbohydrates, but they are easily broken down by your body to give you the power you need right away. Bananas are also well known for being high in potassium, a nutrient that needs to be replenished frequently. This is because potassium is an electrolyte that is lost through stress and heavy exercise. To

further increase the effects of bananas, mix it with protein-rich foods.
2. **Yogurt:** The active ingredient in yogurt that will get you through a home exercise program such as the P90X is magnesium. This nutrient not only helps your body to process carbohydrates and proteins needed for energy, but is also helps to release that energy into the body properly. This is why it is a great addition to bananas. If you don't care for yogurt, try things such as cheese and skimmed milk that are low in harmful fats.
3. **Oatmeal:** There is a reason this food is eaten most often at breakfast time. This food contains important components that will lengthen the life of your body's energy sources. Therefore, consuming oatmeal will ensure you have enough get-up-and-go to make it past your high-level home workout and through to your next meal with ease. The vitamin B found in this power food also helps convert carbohydrates. As an added benefit, large flake oats contain low GI carbs that take longer to digest so that it lengthens the lifespan of it's nutrients and keeps you fuller longer.
4. **Green Tea:** You probably know about the great antioxidant properties of green tea, but did you know that the EGCG antioxidant it contains causes your body and mind to work more efficiently? This means that a home workout like the P90X will be more effective. Green tea is a great way to keep hydrated as well. This will help your body regulate its

temperature, move energy through your muscles, and prevent you from wearing yourself out.

5. **80% Dark Chocolate:** Chocolate does contain some caffeine and sugars, but the health and energy benefits are fantastic when you eat small amounts of it each day. The high level of cocoa contains an abundance of antioxidants and compounds such as phenylethylamine that can provide you with long-lasting energy for a home exercise program like the P90X that requires an abundance of energy. It also helps your body to process other nutrients, raise your iron levels, and other pleasant side effects involving the hormone dopamine.

These power foods will give you the nutrients you need to continue through your day after an intense home workout. You won't have to deal with fatigue, which will not only make you feel better but will help you keep up the momentum for your home exercise program.

Now that we have determined what you should be eating, its time to move on to the other questions. Why are you eating? Are you eating because you're hungry, or because you're bored? The leading cause of overeating is boredom. A lot of people also overeat because food is readily available to them in their pantry, often unhealthy food. A simple but helpful method in eliminating unnecessary eating temptations is to simply refrain from buying unhealthy foods or snacks at the grocery store and filling your kitchen with them. Try not to go grocery shopping when you are hungry and more likely to buy unhealthy snack and desserts! Go grocery shopping when you have a full stomach and you're more likely to remain disciplined in purchasing healthy, energy-based options. When you are surrounded by food and have an abundance of snacks in your kitchen, you are more susceptible to eat it. If you feel you need to eat during the day then make sure it's a responsibly sized serving, and put the rest of the food supplies out of sight. Seeing the food will unconsciously make you want more.

When are you eating? If you have a set schedule you are more likely to eat more than you should. Sometimes you body is not hungry at 12 o'clock when it is you lunch break, or 7 o'clock when dinner is ready daily. Eat when you are hungry and only when you are hungry. This helps to prevent over-eating. How about at a party? Snacks are everywhere; you mindlessly just pick up everything and wolf it down as you are having a good time. Stay mindful of your snack consumption! Small snacks add up to your overall fatigue.

Remember, eating foods that give you a steady level of energy will help you through your day. Sometimes it is not easy to keep up with these good eating habits and at other times, we just feel so lifeless and have no energy. Try the healthy aforementioned snacks. They will give you a boost of energy and keeps their level throughout the day.

CHAPTER 4

THE ENERGY 'DIET'

As mentioned repetitiously in this book, the best way to eat to keep up your energy levels is to follow a healthy, balanced diet.

The Eatwell Guide shows the different types of food and drink we should consume and in what proportions to have a healthy, balanced diet.

The main recommendations are to:

- eat at least 5 portions of a variety of fruit and vegetables every day
- base meals on potatoes, bread, rice, pasta or other starchy carbohydrates choose wholegrain versions where possible
- have some dairy or dairy alternatives such as soya drinks choose lower-fat and lower-sugar options
- eat some beans, pulses, fish, eggs, meat and other protein including 2 portions of fish every week, 1 of which should be oily

- choose unsaturated oils and spreads, and eat them in small amounts
- drink 6 to 8 glasses of fluid a day

Eat at regular intervals: If you eat at regular times, you may find it easier to sustain your energy levels.

Try to eat 3 meals a day. Have a healthy snack, such as fruit or low-fat yogurt, between meals if necessary.

Don't skip breakfast: A healthy, balanced breakfast will help keep you going until lunchtime. Despite this, up to a third of us regularly skip breakfast according to the British Dietetic Association (BDA).

Go for healthier options, such as:

- porridge made with lower-fat milk or water, and topped with fruit
- Low-sugar, high-fibre breakfast cereals such as bran or wheat biscuits
- boiled or poached eggs, with wholemeal toast and low-fat spread

If you can't face eating as soon as you get up, take a low-sugar snack to eat on the go, such as fruit.

Aim for at least 5 A Day

Most people eat too much fat, sugar, and salt, and not enough fruit and vegetables.

Fruit and vegetables are good sources of vitamins, minerals and fiber essential nutrients that your body needs to function properly.

Try to incorporate at least 5 portions of a variety of fruit and veg into your daily diet. They can be fresh, frozen, canned, dried or juiced.

Starchy carbohydrates can help sustain energy

Starchy carbohydrates are an important part of a healthy diet. They're a good source of energy and the main source of a range of essential nutrients. Starchy carbohydrates include:

- potatoes
- bread
- cereals
- pasta
- rice

Starchy foods should make up just over a third of what you eat.

Where possible, go for wholegrain or wholemeal varieties, as these are also higher in fibre and will keep you fuller for longer.

Iron-rich foods

Being low in iron can lead to iron-deficiency anaemia, which can make you feel tired and run down.

Teen girls and young women are especially at risk because they lose iron during menstruation.

While red meat, green vegetables and fortified foods such as breakfast cereals are good sources of iron, the important thing is to eat a range of foods to get enough iron.

Healthy drinks

Make sure you stay hydrated by drinking plenty of fluids – the government recommends 6 to 8 glasses every day. This is in addition to the fluid we get from the food we eat.

Water, lower-fat milk, and sugar-free drinks are healthier choices.

Watch your alcohol intake. Alcohol can not only dehydrate you but also disturb your sleep, leading to tiredness the next day.

Cut down on sugar

Adults and children in the UK eat too much sugar. While it does give you a rush of energy, this wears off quickly. It's also bad for your teeth and can be bad for your waistline too! There are sugars in lots of foods, including fruit and vegetables, but you don't need to avoid these types of natural sugars.

However, we should cut down on foods with lots of added sugar, such as:

- sweets
- cakes
- biscuits
- sugary fizzy drinks
- chocolate
- sugary breakfast cereals
- Superfoods and supplements

No single food including those labelled "superfoods", can compensate for unhealthy eating. Most people don't need to take vitamin supplements to improve their energy levels. They can get all the vitamins and minerals they need by eating a healthy, balanced diet.

However, there are some groups of people who are at risk of deficiency and may be advised to take a supplement.

How to Boost Your Energy Level Without Caffeine or Other Stimulants

Do you lack the energy you need to make it through the day? Do you come home from work so exhausted that all you can do is plop down in front of the TV? If you answered yes to these questions, take heart in the fact that you are not alone. Many people are suffering from a lack of energy these days. Stress, poor diet choices and sedentary lifestyle are a few of the major contributing factors to your lack of energy. So if you want to learn how to naturally increase your energy, keep reading as we unravel the mysteries of natural energy boosters.

One of the first things you should do before you try any natural energy remedy is to pay your doctor a visit. Have a complete check up, including blood work, to make sure that a medical condition is not the cause of your lack of energy. Sometimes thyroid conditions or other medical problems can cause you to be tired all the time. So if you get a clean bill of health from your doctor, you can try some of the following natural energy boosters.

Herbal supplements can be great energy boosters. There are many on the market that claims to boost your energy levels. Ginseng is one supplement that has been shown to increase energy levels and improve mental alertness. It is a good idea to research herbal supplements on your own and find out which ones would work for you. But there are other ways to increase your energy level without taking supplements.

Getting plenty of sleep will do a lot for your energy level. Our busy and stressful lives don't leave a lot of time for rest. But your body needs down time to re-cooperate. So a good night's sleep is a must if you want to feel energized the next day. Avoid bright lights such as your cell phone or tv screen an hour before bed. Try to avoid stimulating video games and tv shows and wind down with a book before you sleep. The purchase of a sleep mask will go a long way in blocking out any sunlight that may wake you up prematurely in the morning. You may also want to invest in some sleeping earplugs if your spouse or family members snore!

It is also critical that you watch what you put into your body if you want to maintain a high energy level while staying hydrated. Stay away from trying to boost your energy level and maintain it over long periods with caffeine. You will just crash later. Another downside of caffeine is that it is a diuretic, which means that too much can dehydrate you. Dehydration can zap your energy levels very fast. So instead of high caffeine drinks, start drinking more water to hydrate your cells and energize your body.

It is also important that you get more exercise. It may seem hard to exercise when you are so tired, but the more exercise that you do, the more energy you will have. The body was not meant to be stationary. It was designed to move, so following a good exercise program will boost your energy level and make you feel better.

So if you find yourself dragging through the day, try some of these natural energy boosters. When you give your energy level a boost, you can feel like a kid again!

CHAPTER 5

BOOST YOUR ENERGY WITH COMPLEX CARBOHYDRATES IN YOUR DIET

Without a doubt, most individuals would want to have high energy levels just to perform effective exercise routines to have the ideal body shape they wish for. Usually, they excessively work out until their bodies become worn out and then take the necessary rest time to heal and grow muscle (if that is their goal). But, how do they endure all of those exercises if they have low energy levels?

In order to stay fit and healthy, one must not only take into consideration having a consistent exercise routine, but one also has to consider a healthy diet. Eating is not a hindrance for a person who wants to have a perfectly shaped body. Eating is an integral part of this process. Eating complex carbs for energy is one way of enduring longer workouts.

We often hear most people saying that in order to have the ideal body shape, one must limit his or her food intake. However, according to most research it is not recommended. Our body needs food for energy, nevertheless, instead of limiting food intake, these people should try implementing a healthy diet. Limiting food intake whilst working out strenuously can cause you to quickly become over-worked and weak. Your ability to lift heavier weights and run longer distances will be greatly diminished. It will also bring on great fatigue.

What are Carbohydrates?

Carbohydrates are a macronutrient that provides the body energy to endure the activities of daily living. Carbohydrates are created from carbon dioxide and water through the process of photosynthesis in plants. Thus, carbohydrates are found in most plant sources and are an energy source in organisms. According to research, the only non-plant sources of carbohydrates are milk and milk products.

Basic Forms of Carbohydrates

1. *Sugar:* Sugar is a simple carbohydrate which is usually absorbed in the bloodstream. Sugars are needed by the body cells in the form of glucose in order to perform such bodily processes as digestion. Sugars can either be:

    a. Monosaccharide- single sugar
    b. Disaccharide-double units or sugar

2. *Starch:* This is commonly known as a complex carbohydrate. It is a chain of sugar that is quickly digested by the body needed for energy. It is believed

that complex carbs and energy are directly proportional. This means that if there is an increase of complex carbs, there will also be an increase in the energy level in our body. This especially helps those who are working out.

3. *Dietary Fiber:* This is the most complex form of carbohydrate. It can be soluble or insoluble.

Although carbohydrates come in different forms, they are still functionally similar. Carbohydrates are readily transformed to energy needed for any physical activity and basic body processes. According to research, one gram weight of carbohydrates yields 4 kcal of physical energy. Carbohydrate consumption also spares digesting proteins for energy, since the latter plays an important role in building and repairing worn out muscle tissue which can help with burning fat for energy. Lastly, carbohydrates such as sugars may have a laxative effect.

The Benefits of Complex Carbohydrates

Complex carbohydrates provide the body some of what it needs to operate at peak performance. Here are a few reasons to choose complex carbohydrates over simple carbohydrates.

Fuel: Complex carbs keep the body fueled for an extended period of time. Reaching for simple carbohydrates may be a quick way to fill your stomach or to fulfill a craving, but the simple sugars are speedily digested, resulting in fleeting satiation and hunger returning sooner.

Digestion: Complex carbohydrates take longer to digest. This makes them the key to fulfilling hunger as well as providing a longer lasting source of energy. Because complex carbohydrates often have lots of fiber, this bulks up ones stool, allowing it to move smoothly through the digestive tract. When this occurs, less bloating and gas exist, constipation can be lessened, and more toxins are removed from the body.

Weight Loss: Yes, the right carbs can actually help you lose weight, not gain weight. Eating complex carbohydrates helps you feel full for a longer period of time. As a result, cravings are lessened and the need to reach for unhealthy snacks between planned meals is diminished.

Instead of reaching for a simple carbohydrate, snacking on a complex carb is an easy way to stay on track with your weight loss or maintenance goals.

Heart Health: A diet rich in vegetables has been proven to lower LDL cholesterol and help prevent heart attacks by lowering blood pressure. Complex carbs can keep your heart healthy. Whole grains and legumes also protect the heart by lowering cardiovascular and coronary heart disease risk.

How to Include More Complex Carbs in Your Diet

In order to achieve the benefits of eating more complex carbohydrates, it might be necessary to make some changes to your diet. Here are some examples of easy substitutions:

Instead of white bread and pasta, switch to whole grain bread and pasta. If the switch is intimidating at first, try mixing half whole grain and half white when making pasta.

Other alternatives to pasta are spaghetti squash and zucchini noodles (or zoodles).

- Instead of munching on potato chips, try nuts and raw vegetables.
- Instead of white rice, consider brown rice, quinoa, or beans as a base for dishes.
- Instead of potatoes, try some mashed or roasted cauliflower.
- Instead of instant oatmeal in the morning, try steel-cut oats or rolled oats. Instant oatmeal tends to come with added sugar, while steel-cut or rolled oats are more natural.

Complex Carbohydrates as Energy

In general, carbohydrates are undeniably the important source of energy for most athletes and people who exercise. Carbs provide energy in order to stimulate the muscles to contract. Ingested carbohydrates will be broken down into simple sugars, such as glucose, fructose and galactose that are easily stored and used as energy. Glucose not used by the body will be stored in the muscles and the liver in the form of glycogen. Excess glycogen will also be stored as fat.

Unlike simple carbohydrates, complex carbs take longer to digest and be absorbed by the body. It also takes a longer time to metabolize; thus, energy to be provided is very slow releasing compared to simple sugars. As mentioned earlier, both starch and dietary fiber are examples of complex carbs, but it is proven that starch is the best source of energy needed by athletes because it is metabolized and is being stored as glycogen.

Change the Reputation of Carbs

In the end, complex carbohydrates are the opposite of fattening. Rather, they're filling, providing our bodies with nutrients it will appreciate. The ability to feel fuller longer will help prevent an unnecessary consumption of sugar, which can be harmful to our blood sugar levels. This makes complex carbs a win-win for everyone who chooses spaghetti squash over a box of macaroni at night.

CHAPTER 6

RAW FOOD DIET

It is important for each of us to evaluate the role that food plays in our daily lives. What kind of toxins are we consuming? Are we getting enough nutrients? Does our body have enough energy to get us through the day? Eating raw foods can help answer these questions and more.

How Raw Foods Heal Our Body

Food is nothing more than fuel for our bodies. Many of us elevate food to a place of emotional significance. Though sharing a meal can certainly provide a stimulating social experience, ultimately food is nothing more than how we keep our bodies running smoothly and effectively. So, what does it mean if we fill our bodies with the wrong kind of fuel? What if the fuel we put in our bodies is actually harmful or toxic? Then, the system begins to breakdown and our bodies begin to show signs of disease.

This diet review will show us that by going back to basics, by filling our bodies with the kinds of food it has relied on for thousands of years, we can reduce disease, lose weight, increase energy and overcome a reliance on toxic foods that only serve to make our bodies sick.

Specific Nutritional Requirements

From a biological standpoint, our body is made up of billions of cells. Each cell has a unique function and relies on specific nutritional elements for maximum efficiency. These foods, especially organic fruits, are full of beneficial enzymes, proteins, amino acids, vitamins and minerals; precisely the nutrients that our cells need for healthy function.

When food is cooked, the nutrients are broken down at an alarming rate. The use of high-heat cooking methods not only destroys enzymes, vitamins and minerals, but it can also lead to increased carcinogens and toxins in an otherwise healthy food.

You will find that almost any popular health journal has conducted a raw food diet review in response to the growing epidemic of poor health and increased disease in our society. Research consistently shows that consuming large amounts of these vegetables and fruits can reduce your risk for cancer, heart disease, obesity and reduce the severity of symptoms for diseases such as arthritis and fibromyalgia.

The best rule of thumb for a raw diet is the 80-10-10 rule: at least 80% of your diet should be vegetables and fruit with no more than 10% being protein or 10% fat.

Eating a diet rich in natural, raw foods, along with a modest amount of raw seeds and nuts, is like giving our body exactly what it needs for optimal function and efficiency. If the cells in our body are happy, we feel good, our mood improves and our energy increases.

What Foods Can A Raw Food Diet Include?

Raw diet foods such as vegetables, especially a food like broccoli which contains high Vitamin C and folate, is an excellent choice of a raw food. Oxygen Radical Absorbance Capacity or often just called ORAC value is higher in a food such as spinach, nuts, blueberries, strawberries. These types of foods have a high ORAC value, though it can be lowered or completely diminished by cooking.

Raw Food Diet Tips - That WILL Boost Your Energy

Here are 3 Proven Raw Food Diet Tips- That WILL Boost Your Energy, Metabolism and Help You Lose Weight For Good:

1. *Eating raw foods is a proven way to eat for more energy*: If you have health challenges then this may be for you. Your body has the incredible natural intelligence of being able to heal almost anything (within reason). However, you must provide your body with the essential elements it needs to heal. You can heal many illnesses and ailments with natural foods.

2. *You crave what's in your blood, therefore you must change what's in your blood*: Avoid sugars, fast foods and processed foods. They are addictive, causing you to come back for more and more. That's just what the big food conglomerates want - you to be addicted to their modified food and for their wealth to grow.

3. Abolish your cravings. Your body is starving for alkalinity: Most people eat dead (over-cooked, over-processed) acid-forming foods. Eating dead food predisposes your body to food allergies, slow metabolism and increased hyperactivity, causing you to put on weight and not look and feel your best. Raw green leafy foods and whole foods are naturally alkaline. Alkalinity also discourages cancer cell growth. Cancer has an extremely difficult time growing in a body that is fueled by healthy, raw, green foods.

What It Will Do For You?

1. Look Better (get that outer glow) and Feel better (raw healthy foods improve mood)
2. Increased Energy and higher libido
3. Detoxify and cleanse to get rid of the "bloat" or "bulge" feeling
4. Better athletic endurance

3-Step Easy Raw Food Recipe Tips- for busy people on the go:

1. Get the best organic vegetables and fruits, nuts and seeds
2. Prepare bite size pieces (kids love this, they can help in the kitchen!), place in baggies ready- to-go for work or school

3. Blend smoothies or green drinks - place in to-go cooler

Once a week, I will prepare my weekly smoothie ingredients in Tupperware containers and freeze them. To each of the seven Tupperware containers I will add the following ingredients; (All organic) Spinach, kale, half a banana, half an apple, ginger, turmeric. The following morning I will add the frozen ingredients to my blender. Before blending I will add a spoonful of organic coconut oil, vegan protein powder, a spoonful of matcha green tea and I will pour on a mixture of grains, often hemp seeds, chia seeds or a combination bag. I will then blend with some almond milk or water. This gives me monstrous energy throughout the day! I will usually consume my daily smoothie after juicing on an empty stomach first thing in the morning.

It is important to purchase a quality blender that has the power to blend frozen ingredients and can sustain long periods of durability.

I personally recommend the **Oster Blender | Pro 1200 - https://amzn.to/2SXTs7P**

I use this product every day and can attest to its durability and excellent performance!

Before consuming my smoothie I will ingest a coffee mug filled with raw vegetable juice first thing in the morning on an empty stomach (after chugging plenty of water to hydrate my cells of course! I create a daily vegetable juice cocktail out of (organic) celery, cucumber, broccoli, and sometimes kale stalks (if I have added the kale leaves to my prepared smoothies the night before and have the stalks leftover in the fridge). I sometimes add carrots to my juice cocktails, although I avoid them where possible so as to not intake excess sugar. You can also juice fruit although I recommend sticking with vegetables to avoid the excess sugar. If you want to get your kids to juice also, then try adding in an organic apple or orange to cover up the earthy taste of the vegetable juice. They will love the taste and be getting a dose of wonderful nutrients that they will not find in the shelved juices. Try to juice the vegetables day-of and consume within twenty minutes as there are valuable enzymes and nutrition found in the newly made juice that will begin to perish the moment it touches the air. You will miss out on these energy-boosting nutrients if you rely on store-bought, pre-made juices. I often wash the vegetables and fill a Tupperware container with them the night before and stick them in the fridge, ready to go for the morning. Just like the blender, you must make sure that you purchase a high quality juicing that can sustain long periods of durability.

I recommend the **Mueller Austria Juicer Ultra 1100W Power, Easy Clean Extractor Press Centrifugal Juicing Machine - https://amzn.to/32nt9uR**

I use this product every morning and can attest to its durability, high quality and convenience of easy cleaning due to the simple removable parts.

I can safely say that preparing smoothies and juicing daily has skyrocketed my energy levels, increased my happiness and sense of wellbeing, and improved the quality of my entire life. I also look younger and no longer suffer from fatigue!

You will love that you can slowly incorporate the raw food diet into your own lifestyle. You do not necessarily have to eat all raw foods, but adding more of them into your diet will be very beneficial for you and your families health.

How to Adopt a Raw Food Diet

If your health is important to you and you have done a raw food diet review and researched the benefits of eating raw, then incorporating raw eating habits into your lifestyle is the next step towards optimum well being.

But how do you get started? First, start by incorporating more organic fruit into your daily routine. Go out on a limb and try a few new varieties you have never had before. The more varied your diet, the more creative you can be with your meal planning down the road.

A healthy raw food diet should make you feel stronger and more energetic within a few weeks. Many people start their raw food journey with a detoxification period in order to purge all of the toxins from their body for a fresh start. If you still have questions or if you would like to continue to learn more about the raw food lifestyle as your move forward, consider purchasing a few raw food diet books and find online resources and support forums that allow you to connect with other raw food lovers.

Once you have an understanding of the basics of a raw food diet, you can move to eating one raw meal each day. As raw fruits and vegetables become a larger part of your daily routine, you will find it easy to expand your recipes and techniques to include countless alternatives for some of your favorite dishes.

Health For Life

With a little additional planning and know-how, anyone can adopt a healthy raw food diet. Though adopting the diet is simple enough, it is important to pay close attention to your calcium, iron and vitamin B-12 intake to avoid deficiencies. Variety is the key to a nutritious and healthy diet, so diversify your fruits and learn how to sprout grains and legumes for additional nutritional supplements.

Even if you do not adopt entirely this diet, simply replacing a meal or two per day with these foods can have tremendous health benefits and reduce toxins in your body. It is important to stay on top of the latest news and research, so you should consider subscribing to health journals or medical blogs that will provide regular raw food diet review details and studies.

The Raw Food Diet Benefits

Many people are now using the Raw Food Diet as a way to improve their health and to help them lose weight.

Certainly, those who have used this diet before or who still use it now have found it extremely beneficial for health and weight loss issues and goals.

With this particular diet one cannot eat any foods which are either processed or which have been cooked, and as the name "The Raw Food Diet" suggests; all foods are eaten in a raw state. One will be required to eat foods such as fresh vegetables, fruit, sprouts, seeds, nuts, beans, grains, seaweed, and dried fruit also.

It is believed that once food has been heated above 116 degrees Fahrenheit, most of the enzymes contained within the food (that aid digestion and help the body to absorb nutrients) are destroyed. It is also thought that through cooking, the essential nutrients that our bodies need and get from food are destroyed as well.

In order for you to be truly using a raw food diet, around 75% of all that you eat should be living or in a raw state. These diets contain far less trans and saturated fats in them and also the levels of sodium within the foods are much lower. This is a diet that ensures that levels of potassium, magnesium, folate and fiber are increased as well as providing the body with phytochemicals (biologically active compounds in plants that stimulate our immune systems, prevent foods from becoming carcinogens in our bodies and reducing inflammation that can help cancer grow).

When eaten in the aforementioned amounts, raw foods reduce the risk of a person contracting such diseases as diabetes, cancer or heart disease. This raw food diet has been the subject of several studies. Details of which have been published in the Journal of Nutrition which showed that a raw food diet lowered the levels of cholesterol and triglyceride (a type of fat found in the blood that can raise the risk of heart disease) in the body.

Although many may argue that implementing such a diet will help you, there are plenty of others who do.

Certainly for those who believe in this diet and used it they have found it to have been extremely beneficial to them. The main health benefits to a person who uses the raw food diet along with reducing the chance of heart disease and losing weight it has other ones as well such as:-

1. A person's energy levels increase.
2. As time progresses the condition of their skin improves.
3. Their digestive system works far better, thus, decreasing fatigue.

As well as being beneficial to one's health, through eating raw foods, you find that these foods often have much more flavor than those which have been cooked. You may find that you don't need to add spices, salt or sugar or any other kinds of condiments to them to improve their flavor. These types of ingredients can actually irritate ones digestive system and stimulate other organs to work excessively in the body.

I often eat a salad for lunch consisting of raw, organic arugula, spinach, kale and some almond sprinkled on top. I will use a half shot of apple cider vinegar on top for dressing. This makes for a delicious and incredibly healthy raw, vegan salad! I will have at least one of these salads a day for lunch a few hours after my morning green smoothie and juicing session.

With the raw food diet, what you are eating is of a much better quality then processed foods and often you find you need to eat far less of it in order to meet your body's nutritional requirements.

The more raw food you eat then the more satisfied you will feel. This provides your body with the energy it needs.

A good raw food diet for health and weight loss is one that consists of a good balance of nutrients, fiber and water to help meet the needs of your body so it functions at its optimum levels.

CONCLUSION

Thank you again for downloading this book!

I hope this book was able to help you start eating for more energy, which will allow you be in a position of knowledge that will allow you to derive a number of benefits. This will enable you to dip into the secrets that will be very useful in melting away your body fat and ensure you maintain a healthy body.

Ultimately, if you decide to start focusing on energy while eating, you will be proud that you made the decision to purchase this book. You will have a stronger body to work with, a leaner body that looks its best and be assured of excellent health. That will come as no surprise as the concepts behind eating for more energy discussed in this book are extremely effective and time tested.

The next step is to choose your daily eating habits and win the battle against fat by losing weight as well as quickly melting your body fat. One way to make sure that you can achieve this is by adopting the process of eating for MAXIMUM DAILY ENERGY.

Finally, if you enjoyed this book, then I'd like to ask you for a favor, would you be kind enough to leave a review for this book on Amazon? It'd be greatly appreciated!

Go to this web address to leave a review for 'Energy Diet: How To Eat For Maximum Daily Energy'!

https://amzn.to/2VqexJw

Thank you and good luck!

www.ingramcontent.com/pod-product-compliance
Lightning Source LLC
Chambersburg PA
CBHW071916070526
44583CB00016B/2016